IR

SOCCER SOURCE

SOCCER'S SUPERSTARS

THE BEST OF THE BEST

Amanda Bishop

CRABTREE
Publishing Company
www.crabtreebooks.com

Dedicated
by Margaret Salter to Shlomi Zlicha
for being an all around superstar

Author
Amanda Bishop

**Publishing plan research
and development**
Kelly McNiven

Editors
Rachel Stuckey, Kelly McNiven

Proofreader and indexer
Natalie Hyde

Photo research
Melissa McClellan

Design
Tibor Choleva

Prepress technician
Margaret Amy Salter

Print and production coordinator
Margaret Amy Salter

Consultant
Sonja Cori Missio, International
  soccer correspondent, featured
  in The Guardian, Forza Italian
  Football, and Soccer Newsday

Photographs
Keystone Press: © DPA (p 6); © Pam Royal (p 7 top); © Brian Peterson (p 12);
  © Imago (p 13 top); © John Walton (p 20); © Pic-Agency Sweden (p 25 top);
  © Larry C. Lawson (p 28 bottom)
Zumapress.com/Keystone Press: © Robin Parker (p 16); © Werek (p 15 bottom);
  © Yorick Jansens (p 17 top); © Hitoshi Mochizuki (p 19); © Michael Mangum
  (p 21); © Alan Schwartz (p 22); © Ot,Ibrahim (p 26); © Ed Sykes (p 29 top)
Alamy: © Trinity Mirror / Mirrorpix (p 27 right)
Associated Press: © Robson Fernandjes (p 8);AP Photo/Bippa (p 10)
SuperStock: © Marka (p 11 top, 14); © Richard Wareham (p 24)
Getty Images: © Lars Baron (p 15)
dreamstime.com: © Photographerlondon (p 5 bottom, p 30)
Shutterstock.com: © Natursports (titlepage, p 9 bottom; 14–15 top, 22–23 bottom,
  25 bottom, 28–29 bottom, 29 bottom); © katatonia82 (p 3, 8–9 top); © Laszlo
  Szirtesi (p 4); © Andreas Gradin (p 7 bottom); © Celso Pupo (8–9 bottom);
  photoplanet.am (p 11 bottom); © Maxisport (p 13 bottom, 17 bottom); © Pavel L
  Photo and Video (14–15 bottom, 22–23 top); © Photo Works (p 18, 28 top);
  © Rui Alexandre Araujo (p 23); © Mitch Gunn (p 27 left); © Vladymyr Mogyla
  (28–29 top)
Public Domain: p 5 top; p 9 top
Wikipedia Creative Commons: © Reindertot (p 9 left)
© Photosport.com: front cover

Created for Crabtree Publishing by BlueApple*Works*

Cover: Champions of the Women's Professional Soccer league in the U.S.
Title page: Gerard Pique celebrates the winning goal during the Spanish Super
Cup final match between FC Barcelona & Real Madrid.

Library and Archives Canada Cataloguing in Publication

Bishop, Amanda, author
    Soccer superstars : the best of the best / Amanda Bishop.

(Soccer source)
Includes index.
Issued in print and electronic formats.
ISBN 978-0-7787-0243-6 (bound).--ISBN 978-0-7787-0252-8 (pbk.).--
ISBN 978-1-4271-9433-6 (pdf).--ISBN 978-1-4271-9429-9 (html)

    1. Soccer players--Biography--Juvenile literature. 2. Soccer
teams--Juvenile literature. I. Title.

GV942.7.A1B58 2013   j796.334092'2   C2013-905779-X
                                               C2013-905780-3

Library of Congress Cataloging-in-Publication Data

Bishop, Amanda.
  Soccer's superstars : the best of the best / Amanda Bishop.
    pages cm. -- (Soccer source)
  Includes index.
  ISBN 978-0-7787-0243-6 (reinforced library binding : alk.
paper) -- ISBN 978-0-7787-0252-8 (pbk. : alk. paper) -- ISBN
978-1-4271-9433-6 (electronic pdf : alk. paper) -- ISBN 978-1-
4271-9429-9 (electronic html : alk. paper)
  1. Soccer players--Juvenile literature. 2. Soccer teams--
Juvenile literature. I. Title.

GV942.7.A1B57 2014
796.334092'2--dc23
[B]
                                            2013033223

Crabtree Publishing Company

www.crabtreebooks.com   1-800-387-7650

Printed in Canada/092013/BF20130815

Published in Canada
Crabtree Publishing
616 Welland Ave.
St. Catharines, Ontario
L2M 5V6

Published in the United States
Crabtree Publishing
PMB 59051
350 Fifth Avenue, 59th Floor
New York, New York 10118

Published in the United Kingdom
Crabtree Publishing
Maritime House
Basin Road North, Hove
BN41 1WR

Published in Australia
Crabtree Publishing
3 Charles Street
Coburg North
VIC 3058

CONTENTS

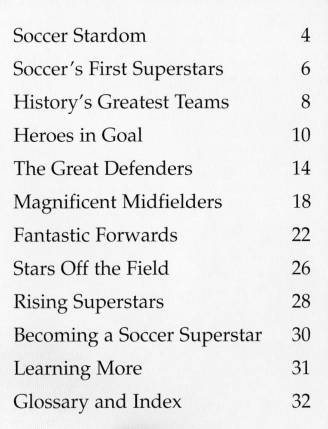

SOCCER STARDOM

Soccer's **superstars** are the very best players in the game. Their abilities and performance on the field set them apart. Top **club** teams are packed with stars brought in from all over the world. When star players appear on their national teams in **international tournaments** like the FIFA World Cup, the home crowd goes wild!

Soccer superstars play in all positions and at every level of competition.

Never Give Up

Competing in the World Cup is a goal for all aspiring soccer superstars. The first World Cup was held in Uruguay in 1930. Uruguay's first goal of the tournament was scored by Héctor Castro, a player who lost his right arm in an accident involving a saw at the age of 13. Most memorably, Castro scored the last goal in the final match of the 1930 World Cup to seal Uruguay's historic victory! He also helped his team win an Olympic gold in 1928.

Fans see the glory of being a superstar, but they may not see all of the hard work that goes into becoming one.

The Makings of a Superstar

There are many **positions** on a soccer team that require speed, strength, and focus. **Forwards** or **strikers** try to score goals in the opposing team's net. **Midfielders** play in the middle of the field, passing the ball forward and slowing down the opponents' **attack**. **Defenders** or **backs** play close to their own net and try to stop the other team from taking shots on goal. **Goalkeepers** or **keepers** protect the net at all costs.

Young stars are often scouted, or invited to play, by clubs who want to help them develop their talent.

Ask anyone who the best male and female soccer players in history are, and you will likely hear about one of these two players: Pelé and Mia Hamm. Both were impressive players from a young age. Their many achievements have inspired soccer fans all over the world.

The Boy from Brazil

Edson Arantes do Nascimento, better known as Pelé, first caught the world's attention at the 1958 World Cup at age 17. He made history by scoring a **hat trick**, or three goals in one game, in the tournament and becoming the youngest player ever to win a World Cup! He went on to play and win two more World Cups. As a forward and attacking midfielder, he scored almost 1300 goals in his career!

FIFA named Pelé the Player of the Century in 2000, along with Diego Maradona.

Marvelous Mia

Mariel "Mia" Hamm joined the United States national women's team at age 15. She was only 19 when the team took home the first Women's World Cup in 1991. As a forward, Mia was a top goal-scorer with a record 158 international goals. In 2004, she was one of two women to make Pelé's list of the top 125 soccer players in celebration of FIFA's 100 year anniversary.

Mia Hamm retired shortly after winning her second Olympic gold medal in 2004.

Women's Soccer Gaining Ground

The future of girls' and women's soccer is bright. But it has taken many years of hard work for soccer's top women to gain opportunities and respect. The first Women's World Cup was held in 1991, more than 60 years after the first men's tournament. Women's soccer did not become an Olympic sport until 1996, some 88 years after men's.

Soccer is one of the most popular sports for girls today.

7

HISTORY'S GREATEST TEAMS

The only thing better than watching a soccer superstar play is watching an entire team of superstars! The best teams have strong players in every position. They work together to produce results.

Brazil's National Team

The Brazilian men's team has won five World Cup championships, more than any other country. After their third win in 1970, FIFA gave the Jules Rimet Cup to Brazil for good. Unfortunately, the solid gold trophy was stolen in 1983 and never seen again. New FIFA rules prevent the trophy from being awarded permanently, so Brazil is the only team to have held this honor.

Brazilian team captain Cafu kisses the trophy after Brazil's fifth World Cup win. The new FIFA World Cup trophy was first awarded in 1974. Winning teams receive a gold-plated version of the trophy to keep, but the original belongs to FIFA.

The Dick, Kerr's Ladies Football Club

When World War I broke out in Europe, many young men left home to fight. Women, who were not allowed to fight, went to work in factories. They kept up spirits in their communities by playing charity soccer matches. The women of the Dick, Kerr & Company **munitions** factory team were unstoppable.

They played a total of 828 games. They won 758, tied 46, and lost only 24!

On December 26th, 1920, the Dick, Kerr's Ladies FC played St. Helen's Ladies FC in Liverpool in front of a record crowd of 53,000 spectators.

Fans of FC Barcelona might argue that their team is the best club team around.

The original Jules Rimet Trophy was named after a former FIFA president.

Great goalkeepers never take their eyes off the ball. They see everything on the field and react. The best keepers are ready to stretch, dive, or leap across the goal to keep the ball out of the net.

Lev Yashin

Lev Yashin was born in 1929 in the former Soviet Union. He was nicknamed the "Black Spider" because he always dressed in black and seemed to have extra arms when making saves. He was one of the first keepers to punch the ball away instead of always trying to catch it. With three World Cup appearances and a 1956 Olympic gold medal, he was named the best goalkeeper of the 20th century by the International Federation of Football History and Statistics (IFFHS).

*Yashin had 270 career **shut-outs**, or games with no goals allowed.*

Gianluigi Buffon

One of Italy's best players, Gianluigi Buffon is captain and goalkeeper for the Serie A team Juventus as well as the Italian national team. In 1996, he played for Italy's winning team in the UEFA U-21 (under 21) championships. Ten years later, Buffon helped lead the country to victory at the 2006 World Cup. He allowed only two goals in the entire tournament! He has won many awards, including the Yashin Award (now called the Golden Glove), awarded to the best keeper of a World Cup tournament.

Gianluigi "Gigi" Buffon is one of Italy's best-loved players.

Hope Solo

American keeper Hope Solo started her soccer career as a forward on her high school soccer team. She switched her position to goalkeeper when she began playing for University of Washington. Since then she went on to play as keeper for leagues in Sweden, France, and the United States. Solo has played with the United States national team since 2000. In 2013, she also joined the Seattle Reign FC in the National Women's Soccer League. She has won Olympic gold twice and appeared in two World Cups.

In 2006, Hope Solo played an impressive streak of 1,054 minutes of game time without allowing a single goal!

Key Keepers

Brazilian keeper Rogéri Ceni has scored a record 111 goals since 1990, which is hard to do from the other end of the field!

Italian Dino Zoff once played 1,143 minutes without letting in a single goal.

In 1999, José Luis Chilavert of Paraguay became the first keeper to score a hat trick in a game for his club team, Vélez Sársfield.

At the 2007 Women's World Cup, keeper Nadine Angerer did not allow a single goal in 540 minutes of play, helping Germany win their second Women's World Cup title.

Nadine Angerer in action

Iker Casillas

Casillas was the captain of Spain's winning team at the 2010 World Cup, where he won the Golden Glove for best keeper of the tournament. He also won the Golden Glove after Spain's 2008 and 2012 Euro victories. Both FIFA and IFFHS named him the world's best keeper from 2008 to 2012.

Iker Casillas has played for Real Madrid in Spain's Primera División, also known as La Liga, for his entire career.

THE GREAT DEFENDERS

The best defenders are fast, sharp, and fearless. It is their job to stop attacks from the opposing team and to keep them as far from the net as possible. They must make good **tackles** and strong passes to move the ball up the field. They even score a goal or two!

Paolo Maldini

Italy's Paolo Maldini was one of soccer's best defensive players. He was known for his size, his strength, and his leadership. When playing, he tried to tackle as little as possible. Instead, he positioned himself on the field to stop attacking players. He played for Serie A team A.C. Milan for his entire career. The team retired his jersey, number 3, in 2009.

Maldini's nickname was "Il Capitano," or "The Captain."

Faye White wore a protective mask in the Euro 2009 final after suffering a broken cheekbone earlier in the tournament.

Faye White

Faye White of England joined the national team at age 16. She went on to captain the team at four major international tournaments. She also played for Arsenal Ladies FC in the Women's Premier League from 1996 to 2013. As team captain, White led Arsenal to fifteen major championship titles.

Did You Know?

Legendary German defender Franz Beckenbauer was known for playing **sweeper**, a defender who plays behind the other defenders and blocks any gaps.

Franz Beckenbauer is regarded as the greatest German soccer player of all time.

Philipp Lahm

While only 5'7" (1.7 m), Philipp Lahm proves that defenders don't have to be giants to be superstars. Lahm's speed and **agility**, or ability to change directions quickly, help him stay with the ball and slow down attacking forwards. He is captain of Bayern Munich of Germany's professional league, Bundesliga. At his first World Cup in 2006, he scored the first goal of the tournament and in 2010, he became the German national team's youngest captain ever.

Philipp Lahm (on the left) has been chosen twice for FIFA's World Cup All-Star Team.

Vincent Kompany

Belgian center back Vincent Kompany started playing for his national team and the Belgian Pro League when he was only 17 years old. In 2008, he moved to Manchester City FC in the English Premier League. Kompany was voted the team's Player of the Year for the 2010-2011 season. The next year, he was named Player of the Season for the entire Premier League. In 2011, he became captain of the Belgian national squad.

In 2013, Vincent Kompany bought a club team in Brussels to create opportunities for young people in his hometown to play soccer.

Dazzling Defense

Between 1993 and 1996, American defender Carla Werden Overbeck played 63 **consecutive** games, or games played in a row, for her national team.

Germany's Lotthar Matthäus and Italy's Fabio Cannavaro are the only two defenders to have won FIFA's World Player of the Year award.

In 1998, defenders Fan Zhiyi and Sun Jihai became the first Chinese players in the Premier League.

Fabio Cannavaro spent the majority of his career in Italy.

17

MAGNIFICENT MIDFIELDERS

Midfielders are often the most **versatile** players on the team. They can fall back to help the defense and shoot forward if they see a chance for a goal or an **assist**. Midfielders manage the play by spotting opportunities, controlling the game's **pace**, or speed, and knowing when to make a move.

David Beckham

England's David Beckham may be soccer's best known player today. He was a strong midfielder known for long-range goals, especially from **corner kicks**. He won titles in four different soccer leagues—the Premier League, La Liga, the Major League in North America, and Ligue 1 in France. He captained the English national team for six years. He retired in 2013.

Homare Sawa

Midfielder Homare Sawa was only 15 when she made her first appearance for the Japanese national team. She went on to play in four Olympic tournaments and five Women's World Cup tournaments. She captained the team for their 2011 World Cup victory. She scored 5 goals in the tournament, won the Golden Ball as top goal scorer, the Golden Shoe as top player, and was named FIFA's Woman's World Player of the Year. After retiring from international competition, she returned to play for her Japanese league team, INAC Kobe Leonessa.

Homare Sawa (center) played in American leagues for many years, but now plays in the Plenus Nadeshiko League in Japan.

Yaya Touré

Hailing from the Côte d'Ivoire (Ivory Coast), Yaya Touré is one of today's top midfielders. He often changes position during games, and is known for his speed and creativity in making goal-scoring opportunities. Touré played in Belgium, the Ukraine, Greece, and France before joining Barcelona FC in 2007. He also played alongside his brother, defender Kolo Touré, for Manchester City FC. The two brothers also played for the Côte d'Ivoire's national team in the 2006 and 2010 World Cup tournaments.

Yaya Touré was named African Footballer of the Year in 2011 and in 2012.

Megan Rapinoe

American midfielder Megan Rapinoe had a long career on the national youth team. She played in U-16 and U-19 tournaments, including the U-19 Women's World Championship in 2004. She played in the 2011 Women's World Cup and the 2012 Olympics, in which the United States won the gold medal. In 2013, she was named Player of the Tournament at the **Algarve Cup**.

Megan Rapinoe played league soccer in the United States before moving to Olympique Lyonnais in France.

Magic in the Midfield

One of the greatest midfielders ever, Zinedine Zidane of France won the FIFA World Player of the Year three times.

Sir Stanley Matthews of England was known as the Wizard of the Dribble for his midfield magic. He retired at age 50—the oldest Premier league player.

In a 2013 Champions League game between FC Barcelona and Paris Saint-Germain FC, Spain's Xavi Hernández completed 96 passes!

Midfielder Jone Samuelson of Norway broke records when he headed a ball 187 feet (57.3 m) up the field—right into the opposing team's empty net!

FANTASTIC FORWARDS

Forwards, or strikers, have a great ability to find their way past the defense and take shots on goal. They play as far forward on the field as they can get without being called **offside**. If they can hit their target when it counts the most, forwards can become national heroes!

Abby Wambach

American Abby Wambach first played for the national team in 2003. Since then, she has appeared in three Women's World Cups and won two Olympic gold medals in 2004 and again in 2012. Wambach has also played in all three women's leagues created in the United States since 2001. She was named the U.S. Soccer Federation's Female Athlete of the Year five times between 2003 and 2011.

In 2012, Abby Wambach was named FIFA's Women's World Player of the Year.

Cristiano Ronaldo

Portugal's Cristiano Ronaldo has won several awards for his achievements on the field, including the FIFA World Player of the Year in 2008. In 2009, he became the most expensive soccer player in history. Ronaldo has played for club teams in Portugal's Primeira Liga, the Premier League, and La Liga. In 2011–2012, he set a La Liga record by scoring at least once against every opposing team in one season.

Cristiano Ronaldo is captain of Portugal's national team.

Did You Know?

Abby Wambach's goal in the 122nd minute of the quarter-final match at the Women's World Cup in 2011 was the latest goal ever scored during World Cup play!

Marta

Many people believe that Brazilian striker Marta Vieira da Silva, known simply as "Marta," is the best female soccer player in the world. She was FIFA's World Player of the Year five times in a row from 2006 to 2010. Marta has played in leagues in Brazil, the United States, and Sweden, and has played in three Women's World Cups and three Olympic tournaments. At the 2007 World Cup, she was awarded both the Golden Shoe and the Golden Ball.

Like many soccer superstars, Marta uses her celebrity for a good cause. She became a Goodwill Ambassador for the United Nations in 2010.

Striking Gold

Argentina's Diego Maradona is known for scoring one of the worst and one of the best goals in World Cup history within moments of one another. In the quarter-final match against England, the English goalkeeper, came out to punch a ball clear of the net. Maradona knocked the first goal in with his own hand, which the referee did not see. The English team protested the goal, but the call stood. A few minutes later, he scored again by dribbling past five English players in what was later called one of the greatest goals of the century.

Diego Maradona playing at a charity game in Rome, Italy, in 2012.

Lionel Messi

Quick-footed Lionel Messi is the captain of Argentina's men's team and plays for FC Barcelona. Many believe he is the greatest player on the field today. In 2005, he was the FIFA U-20 top goal scorer and player of the tournament. He won Olympic gold with Argentina, the Ballon D'Or for Europe in 2009, and the FIFA Ballon D'Or in 2010, 2011, and 2012.

In 2013, Lionel Messi improved on Ronaldo's La Liga record by scoring on every other team in consecutive games during one season.

Not every soccer superstar is known for dribbling, shots, and saves. Coaches, managers, trainers, and officials all have important roles to play. Many of the people who help make soccer great work behind the scenes.

Official Stardom

Soccer officials have to stay in great physical shape. Referees must know all of the rules, and be ready to make judgment calls in tricky situations. Pierluigi Collina of Italy was a fair and effective referee. Before he retired at the age of 45, he had officiated final matches at the Olympics, the Euro Cup, and the World Cup.

Pierluigi Collina was named FIFA's best referee of the year six times in a row!

Changing the Game

Sahar El-Hawary was not allowed to play soccer as a child. Now a college professor, she has worked tirelessly to create opportunities for girls and women to learn, practice, and compete. Today, Dr. El-Hawary is the head of the Egyptian Women's Football Federation and a member of FIFA.

Sir Alex Ferguson was one of the top managers in soccer history. He retired from Manchester United in 2013.

Soccer's Best Friend

Shortly before the 1966 World Cup in England, the Jules Rimet Cup was stolen for the first time from a public exhibition. A week later, David Corbett of London took his dog, Pickles, for a walk. While sniffing around, Pickles found the stolen trophy under a hedge! It was returned to the World Cup organizers in plenty of time for kick-off. Unfortunately, the second time the Cup was stolen in Brazil in 1983, it was never found.

Pickles had a brief career in movies following his time as a national hero.

RISING SUPERSTARS

New superstars are always on the rise. Keep your eye on these up-and-coming players. Their skills will entertain a whole new generation of soccer fans!

Omar Gonzalez

Mexican-American Omar Gonzalez started playing defense for the Los Angeles Galaxy in 2009. He was named Rookie of the Year for the league. Just two years later, he was named MLS Defender of the Year. In 2012, he was the Man of the Match in the MLS Cup final.

Alex Morgan

American striker Alex Morgan scored the winning goal in the U.S. victory at the FIFA U-20 Women's World Cup final in 2008. She also landed key goals in the 2012 Olympics, helping her team to win the gold. In 2012, she was named U.S. Soccer's Athlete of the Year.

Alex Morgan plays for Portland Thorns FC in the Women's Professional Soccer league.

Jessica Clarke

Jess Clarke is a midfielder who played for England's U-15, U-17, and U-19 national teams. She is now a member of the English women's team. Her fantastic dribbling was amazing to watch at the Women's Euro 2009, the 2011 Women's World Cup, and the 2012 Olympics in London.

Jess Clarke (left) has already scored 10 goals for the English national team.

Neymar

By the age of 20, Brazilian sensation Neymar had already been named the South American Footballer of the Year—twice! Neymar won Olympic silver with Brazil in 2012. In the 2013 **Confederations Cup** in Brazil, Neymar was awarded the Golden Ball for the best player of the tournament.

Neymar signed with FC Barcelona in May 2013.

BECOMING A SOCCER SUPERSTAR

There is always room for another soccer superstar! Top players spend time practicing skills, studying tactics, and playing their hearts out. Remember that superstars play in every position on the field. Many take on roles off the field, too.

Good, Better, Best!

All soccer superstars face the challenge of being physically fit. They eat healthy diets, get plenty of exercise, and practice the skills they need to play their positions well. They also trust their coaches and managers to guide and challenge them.

A good coach can help you focus on your strengths and improve areas you need to develop.

LEARNING MORE

Books

Doeden, Matt. *The World's Greatest Soccer Players*. Capstone Press, 2010.

Goldsworthy, Steve and Aaron Carr. *The Greatest Players: Soccer*. Weigl AV2, 2012.

Mackin, Bob. *Soccer the Winning Way*. Greystone, 2001.

Thomas, Keltie. *How Soccer Works*. Owlkids Books, 2007.

Web Sites
The National Women's Soccer League

This web site has match details, statistics, and player profiles of all your favorite players in the United States.

www.nwslsoccer.com

Major League Soccer

The MLS soccer website has all the latest news and video of action in the men's league of North America.

www.mlssoccer.com

FIFA

For the latest information on soccer superstars around the world, the FIFA web site provides information on national teams and upcoming events, including the World and Euro Cups.

www.fifa.com

GLOSSARY

Note: Some boldfaced words are defined where they appear in the book.

Algarve Cup A women's annual international tournament featuring the best female teams from around the world

assist A play, such as a pass, that sets up a goal-scoring opportunity

attack Any attempt to score a goal or create an opportunity to score a goal

club A soccer organization that has one or more teams that compete in regional or national leagues

Confederations Cup A men's tournament in which the top world teams compete held the year before the World Cup

corner kick A kick taken from the corner of the field by an attacking player when a defending player kicks the ball out of bounds beside their net

international tournaments Series of games played by national teams over a set period of time

munitions Materials used for war, such as weapons

offside A player who is closer to the opposing team's goal line than the ball or a player from the opposing team

positions Roles in the team's strategy or a place on the field

tackles Attempts to gain possession of the ball from another player

versatile Able to adapt quickly and be effective in many ways

INDEX